the last most recent thing that happened

photographs by Ron O'Donnell

Essay by Rod Varley
Edited by Liz Smith

A Harewood House Trust/National Museum of Photography, Film & Television Publication
1994

Harewood House Trust
Estate Office
Leeds LS17 9LQ

National Museum of Photography, Film & Television
Pictureville
Bradford BD1 1NQ

Photographs: © Ron O'Donnell
Essay: © Rod Varley, National Museum of Photography, Film & Television
Edited: Liz Smith, Harewood House Trust
Designed: Imelda Kay

ISBN 0-9521021-2-9

First published 1994

Cover Illustration: detail from 'Expulsion from the Garden' 1989

introduction

Ron O'Donnell's pictures are popular among a wide audience. No knowledge of art or photography is required to enjoy his work and this has, ironically, tested critics and historians invited to write or comment upon it. O'Donnell himself compounds the problem. He is an easy going man who wants to please his interviewer by providing some simple yet plausible explanation as to why people find his work accessible. In short he tries to answer the unanswerable.

O'Donnell has said of himself that if he could remember jokes he would probably be a stand-up comedian. An unfulfilled ambition maybe, but this insight only serves to further colour his reputation as 'humorous Scottish artist'. In a wider context, O'Donnell's photographs are more significant than this. His work is regularly exhibited and written about in catalogues, art journals, colour supplements and newspapers. It has been used by the broadcast and advertising media. In 1987 it won the Fox Talbot Prize and is represented in the collections of the National Museum of Photography, Film & Television; Victoria & Albert Museum; Scottish National Gallery of Modern Art; and the Centre Georges Pompidou in Paris. Undoubtedly its cultural cachet has been secured. Meanwhile, O'Donnell stands on the sidelines as the critics teeter on the brink of a new 'art versus photography' debate.

Generalisations abound. It is often presumed the 'photography world' favours O'Donnell's work because it has broken away from the solemn confines of the documentary tradition, but has retained social and political comment. On the other hand, painters sometimes disapprove of his use of the photographic process, deeming it a substitute for art skills. Critics have used his work to illustrate that much abused term Post-Modernism and, sadly, sculptors may not even recognise a kindred spirit.

O'Donnell's work therefore throws into sharp relief many of the changes that have taken place in our understanding of photography, painting, sculpture and society today.

i

Rod Varley
National Museum of Photography, Film & Television

Liz Smith
Harewood House Trust

the last most recent thing that happened

If we step back, we see that the development of photography satisfied a desire for precision and order that artists had struggled to achieve since the Renaissance. Indeed, the fundamental device of photography, the camera obscura (darkened room), was a sixteenth century artist's tool. For centuries they sought ways to place the viewer in a privileged position, to share a vision of what they themselves had seen. When, in the 1830s, William Henry Fox Talbot and Louis Daguerre perfected means by which optically formed images could be preserved, the artist's role was bound to change. Debates over Naturalism versus Realism, of observation or intervention, Science or Art, were all the rage. All these debates reflected the need to organise and catalogue, to 'understand' before enjoyment could be legitimised.

"Now I do not mean to premise that this confusion between Science and Art exists everywhere - it does not. But I feel sure that it exists largely in the ever-increasing body of persons who practise photography. The majority of them have not thoroughly, nay, not even adequately, thought the matter out."

P H Emerson at the Camera Club Conference,
London, 26 March 1899

Outside a relatively small, educated elite, photography has largely been seen as a mundane activity. Today, it is arguable that the wider public's view of photography-as-art has more to do with Ansel Adams and Athena than, say, Emerson, Stieglitz or Cartier-Bresson. This is not a criticism of the former, but an acknowledgment of the failure to promote the others to a wider audience. For most of us, photography is essentially a point-the-camera-press-the-button activity or, if one extends the nineteenth century concept of 'science', it is an objective technology which merely measures and records patterns of light. The creative and manipulative role of the photographer as creator, selector and decision-maker has been marginalised by the apparent simplicity of the process.

The division of art and science in Western culture is a recent one and has, arguably, been very damaging. Until the eighteenth century, most sciences were arts and the divide that now exists is a product of the nineteenth century. Today, we view painting as art and forget that the impetus which created photography belonged to an age when the artist and scientist were one and the same. The most influential thinkers of the Victorian age sought to bring order to our lives. Science equalled progress, progress was positive, positive was modern. In this climate the clinical, technological precision of photography precipitated a reaction in painting which celebrated the hands-on, tactile application of paint and moved away from its slavishly representational role. Whether Impressionism or Cubism, the late nineteenth and early twentieth centuries saw intellectuals and artists attempting to redefine the essence of painting. Consequently, the subject of painting became the process, an exploration of the medium for its own sake.   This tendency became the heart of what we now think of as Modern Art.

But what has any of this to do with Ron O'Donnell? O'Donnell started off painting and drawing. As a young boy he recalls watching television and sketching things like 'Our Wullie' and the Beano. At school he was reported to be 'good at art'. However, in the 1970s he was sidetracked into what he refers to as 'purist' photography; the European tradition of black and white documentary in which Britain, at that time, was steeped. Photography was not art. This was an era in which, if you took the camera seriously, you took documentary photographs. O'Donnell talks of roaming the streets with a little 35mm camera searching for the decisive moment - the Holy Grail of any respectable photographer. However, like many students of the time he was not very good. Decisive moments seemed to pass him by and he finally reached the conclusion that he was not as quick as Henri Cartier-Bresson. In truth he was not as patient and whilst photography was not art, there was an art to photography.

Flying in the face of all the unwritten rules and breaking his vows as a documentary photographer, he started to manipulate his images. At first it was a move away from people to places and objects, such as a butcher's shop or hairdressers. He slowly moved format from 35mm to 2" square, to 6cm x 7cm, to 5" by 4" sheet film. He encountered narrative and humour in the work of American photographer Duane Michals and through another American, Joel Meyerowitz, got lost in the mesmeric detail of the 10"x 8" format.

The detail of the 10" x 8" format he now uses plays a major role in his work. It has a transparency which recalls the initial impact photography must have had over a hundred and fifty years ago. Even knowing that the camera *does* lie, at this level of technical precision it is perceived simply as a witness. A real scene has been fixed in time, made possible by the presence of the camera. It reaffirms all the old myths about the camera simply being a window on the world.   In practical terms, it means O'Donnell's images are photographically friendly. Unless obsessed by philosophical debates around photographic veracity, viewers simply look through the medium onto a fragment of time preserved - a kind of archaeological record. This is very different from painting. The photographic image has a past, an existence prior to the photograph being made. It also has a future: what follows once the camera is taken away?

This fixed reference to a point in time and space is not present in any other form of representational art; even film and video, although sharing certain similarities, are more clearly constructions.   O'Donnell often constructs his narratives in the time and space before and after the photograph was taken. His stories are created in the viewer's imagination because photography allows the subject to have a real sense of existence outside the photograph.   The advent of photography may have threatened the role of art in the nineteenth century, but in O'Donnell's work it is simply used to do what it is best at - fooling the viewer into believing. With digital imaging and multimedia environments now commonplace, it is possible photography will soon be treated with the general scepticism and caution it deserves. If this happens, the photograph's ability to function as a window will be lost and, maybe, to future audiences O'Donnell's pictures will be seen as paintings.

This may be happening already. In Britain, the 1980s have seen art and commerce re-unite. On one hand, as various systems of state support have been eroded, the role of corporate patronage through commission and sponsorship has created new cultural spaces for artists to work in. On the other, creative commercial companies, like advertising agencies and magazine publishers, have actively incorporated and thus contributed to the world of art and popular culture. Their role is one of cultural positioning and opinion forming and artists like O'Donnell have not only borrowed from their creative styles, but have had their own work appropriated as cultural icons.

This blending of market forces with the world of art, the pick-and-mix culture which critics have branded post-Modernism, is a context in which O'Donnell is frequently seen. If Modernity is forward looking and precise, post-Modernity looks back and mixes. Modernism is often criticised for its elitism. Bound by rules it is art about art for people who know about art. O'Donnell sees his art as using the visual to communicate. He produces for people who do not necessarily 'know' about art. Post-Modernism has also attacked the cult of originality. It often invokes other creative works through quoting and pastiche. As artists have always stolen and plagiarised, so originality is perhaps just another invention of Modernism. O'Donnell clearly sees it as a natural activity.

These views, and O'Donnell's willingness to express them, endear his work to those people who share his belief that art should communicate. Not caring whether he is exhibited as a photographer or an artist, he sees himself as a performer. Like all performers he waits patiently in the wings to hear the public laugh along with his view of the world.

The title of this book, and the exhibition it accompanies, is a direct reference to the specific function photography brings to O'Donnell's work - it records the last most recent thing to have happened. Once taken, it immediately becomes a record of a moment past. But what of painting, sculpture, politics, Scotland and humour?

O'Donnell's work is a reflection of our times. He sees himself as a social commentator with environmental and social issues being common themes. Images of discarded waste on a Spanish beach (**The Orange Tree** fig. 12), the destruction of the rain forests (**ZZZZZZZZ** fig. 17) or the tumbling cascade of mineral water bottles (**The Waterfall** fig. 14) are interesting not simply because they articulate society's concerns about the world, but because they reveal aspects of his working method. All three are made from scrap materials whilst **Christmas Tree** (fig. 2) and **The Ante Chamber of Rameses V in the Valley of the Kings** (fig. 3) are unique to the place in which they were made, in both cases decaying tenement buildings in Edinburgh.

As O'Donnell's work develops, he spends less time searching for locations and collecting materials and concentrates more directly on a sculptural approach. His current favoured material is cardboard which he rips, cuts, shapes and paints as necessary. There has also been a greater demand for him to work on specific commissions. At first he was able to combine his own work with the needs of the commissioner, but more recently works have had to conform to specific briefs. This has made O'Donnell realise that he wishes to say certain things in his work and that the commissions are placing constraints upon him.

Just as his work is located in the environmental and social issues of our time, so it is located in Scotland and in his own personal life. He shares with fellow artist and contemporary, Stephen Campbell, a need to be autobiographical, but unlike Campbell who can verge on the obsessive, O'Donnell is whimsical. The icons and symbols of Scotland are there because he was brought up with them, and specific objects feature because of a fondness or familiarity; The Sunday Post in **Nuclear Wasties** (fig. 4), the tartan framed photograph of a young O'Donnell dressed as Davy Crockett in **The Ante Chamber of Rameses V in the Valley of the Kings** (fig. 3).

There is, however, one aspect of childhood that is a little more serious than the jokiness of the comic - his granny. His granny was a Catholic and in her house in Stirling, still lit by gas in the 1970s, she had an old box bed with curtains. O'Donnell was clearly impressed by the iconography of both Catholicism and the bed. The concept of drawing a set of curtains to go to sleep still fascinates him and it figures in many of his pictures. Even in those where physical curtains are absent, the theatrical staginess implied by the framing is very much evident. The religious iconography is less subtle. In **Adam and Eve** (fig. 10) the cherub hovers above the tree of knowledge proffering condoms as Eve tempts Adam with the forbidden fruit. It is unclear whether this is a comment upon the Catholic Church's attitude to contraception or simply a joke.

Ron O'Donnell's journey from drawn cartoon, through 35mm documentary, to large format tableaux seems to be heading towards a moment when the camera may be discarded. Increasingly the installations which are the basis of the photographs are becoming dominant. Parallels between O'Donnell and Calum Colvin or Stephen Campbell are less relevant than, say, with David Mach or George Wyllie. If one has to fall back on a category for O'Donnell's work, it is, for the time being, photography. What is interesting is that, in fifty years, the very same work may well be seen as something else; something which epitomises the re-unification of the science and technology of photography with the skills of the creative communicator in the late twentieth century.

tactical nuclear explosion

'A nuclear explosion can annihilate a whole city, but as these things can land on a sixpence I thought a more homely idea would be a tactical explosion in your own living room.'

30" x 40"

1985

christmas tree

'The idea of humans not opening presents at Christmas is fairly incongruous -
everybody opens presents. So something must have happened here, but no one is
quite sure what.

I did this in a day and interestingly enough went back a couple of days later to find
that the vagrants and winos using the place had not just opened one present, but
all of them, only to reveal empty boxes. They were obviously not daunted by the
first box being empty and continued to open each one to make sure.

My first reaction was "what if the picture hasn't worked out". There is always the
worry that when you get the transparency back from the Lab it won't be right and
you will have to shoot the whole thing again.'

30" x 40"

1986

the ante chamber of Rameses V
in the valley of the kings

' I'm going to be wrapped in this when I die. It seems quite appropriate in a
way, the pharaohs were wrapped in something and I'm going to be wrapped in
this picture.
I was watching Fellini's 'Roma'; the part where they are building the tunnel and
come across the Roman frescos. The archaeologists come in to look at them
and the wind through the tunnel starts to blow all the frescos away. Eventually
there is nothing left on the wall and these people are frantic because they can't
do anything. So the idea of wall paintings in a room has less to do with
Egyptian artifacts than with this idea from Fellini.'

30" x 40"

1987

nuclear wasties

'Nuclear waste is a big problem and so my idea to give it to a conglomerate like Kellogg to turn into a breakfast cereal sounded like a good capitalist move. You get rid of the nuclear waste plus you make a profit and get a free radiation sticker.'

30" x 40"

1987

5   **to see yourself as others see you**

O Jenny dinna toss your head,
An' set your beauties a' abread!
Ye little ken what cursed speed
The blastie's makin!
Thae winks and finger-ends, I dread
Are notice takin!

O wad some Pow'r the giftie gie us
To see oursels as others see us!
It wad frae monie a blunder free us
An' foolish notion:
What airs in dress an' gait wad lea'e us,
And ev'n Devotion!

'To A Louse, on Seeing one on a Lady's Bonnet at Church'.
Robbie Burns c.1784.

48" x 60"
1988

extinct birds and soft leopards

'I was working in a steading in the Pentlands and somehow the ambience of the place seemed to lend itself to doing something quite different. I was reading a book about extinct species and how things evolved and came across a diagram in the shape of a tree.
It's fake fur which I got from a material shop. You get some strange looks when you ask for leopard skin material.'

60" x 48"

1988

expulsion from the garden

'I had seen some pictures of Adam and Eve being expunged from the garden.
All fire and brimstone. I had these old cases in the garage, I think some
belonged to my granny, and I thought "expulsion from the garden, I'd like to do
something like that".'

60" x 48"

1989

the arch of light

'I did this the last day I was in Spain. It was a very simple idea. I wanted to capture something of how I felt about Valencia, it was a really weird place - full of sixties baroque.'

48" x 60"

1989

the apartment

'The studio I had in Valencia was an old shop and all these things were from the apartment I was staying in. I just made the whole thing up. The trouble with working in Spain is that no one helps you do anything, it's always "tomorrow". I just had to do what I could.'

60" x 48"

1989

10

adam and eve

'This piece was made in my garage after seeing some paintings by the German fifteenth century artist Lucas Cranach the Elder. He did loads of Adam and Eves. At least half a dozen that I saw. They all had this great light in the background and I took from him the idea of where the couple should stand.'

60" x 48"

1989

the burning bush

'Everything is Israeli - right down to the cardboard which is from Jaffa boxes. I was teaching in Jerusalem and got some of the students to work with me. They made the Méliès moon. I asked them to do it so there was no rocket. I guess this piece was done just because I was in Jerusalem and had been brought up a Catholic so knew the Old Testament.'

48" x 60"

1989

the orange tree

'This was in Spain. All the junk lying on the sand came from the beach not far from where I was staying.'

60" x 48"

1990

conceptual elephants

'I don't really like conceptual art, but I had seen this empty cardboard box at an exhibition which got me thinking. Because I use cardboard a lot in my work, I thought I would like to make an amorphous lump of it look like something else. I had a load of wet cardboard outside my house and it reminded me a bit of elephant skin.'

60" x 48"
1990

the waterfall

'I started to see a lot of bottled water in Scotland and I couldn't believe that, in a place where it rains all the time, people were actually buying it. Whereas I used to drink out of streams, after Chernobyl I'm not sure I would let my kids do that. So the healthiest waterfall I could think of was one of bottled water.

Nobody in the Montreal gallery where I made the installation wanted to empty the bottles because of the cost. Instead they put the water in the radiators, down cisterns and in kettles. You opened the fridge in the little canteen and there were Evian bottles everywhere.'

48" x 60"

1990

the bed of osiris

'Osiris, God of the Underworld and Sept, God of Lower Egypt fought one another. Sept cut Osiris into fourteen pieces and distributed them far across the known world. Isis, Osiris' wife and sister, vowed to collect the pieces so that Osiris would again be a whole person and be able to travel to the afterlife. Courageously she collected everything but his penis.'

48" x 60"

1990

the bound angel

'The bound angel is not supposed to be me. It's just that the boots were lying around and I thought a modern day angel would probably wear a pair of Converse.'

60" x 48"

1991

17

zzzzzzzz

'This is really a lesson in how to build a rainforest in your garage. A chain saw is one of the most effective ways of cutting it down.'

60" x 48"

1991

adam and eve

'The shapely plastic model came from a lingerie shop which was going out of business. I am always keen on buying these things and on this occasion I was lucky because it was the last one. I had kept it for a long time and never really used it, but it came to Autumn and I thought it would be nice if she was covered with leaves to complement the man covered in money. The tree is a re-hash of the wings from **The Bound Angel**.'

60" x 48"

1992

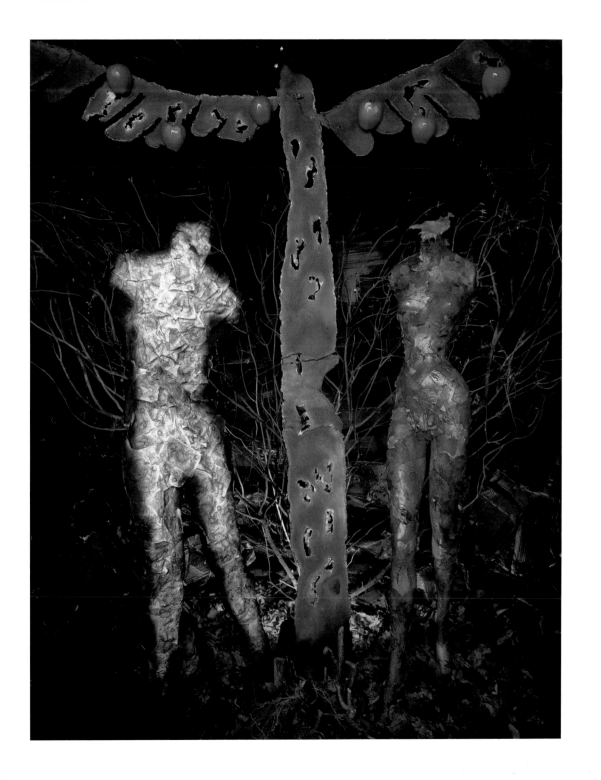

untitled

'This was commissioned by the Scottish Arts Council and Portfolio Gallery during the E.E.C summit held in Edinburgh at Christmas. I was asked to do something on Nationalism so I made two pieces; one with sheep and flags and the hanging Scotland. I remember reading this spoof article in which a Minister said "Why don't we just chainsaw the buggers off and drag them into the North Sea".'

60" x 48"

1992

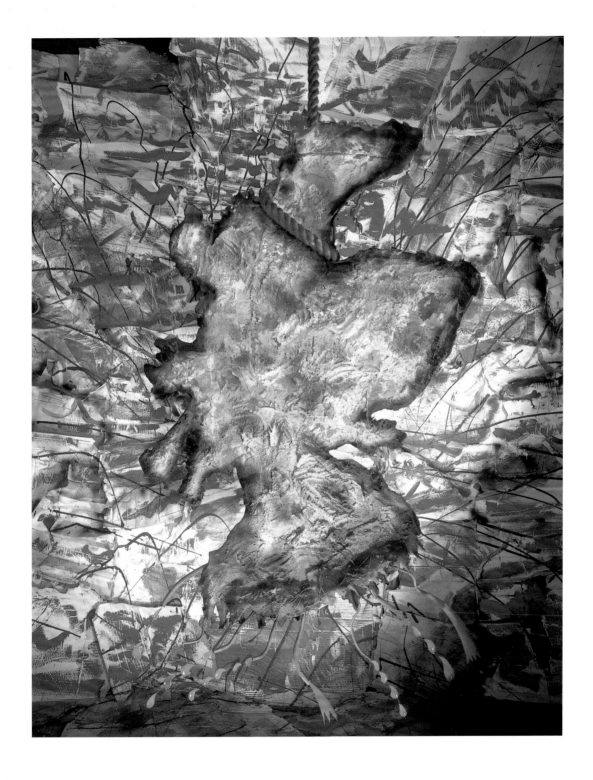

Idea for London Underground poster
(rejected)

60" x 48"

1992

the lovers

London Underground poster

'Commissioned by London Underground, it is a pastiche of the Bronzino in The
National Gallery. My first idea was rejected by the 'Graffiti Committee',
probably because it showed too much flesh. So to overcome the problem I
covered the bodies with images from photographic magazines. This idea was
considered acceptable.'

60" x 40"

1992

Courtesy of London Underground Ltd.

acknowledgements

Harewood House Trust and the National Museum of Photography, Film & Television would like to extend special thanks to Ron and Jackie O'Donnell, Diane Lascelles, Ian Riddell at Warrens Imaging, Chris Pulleine at ABSA, Greg Hobson, Philippa Wright, Imelda Kay and Penny Fell at the National Museum of Photography, Film & Television.